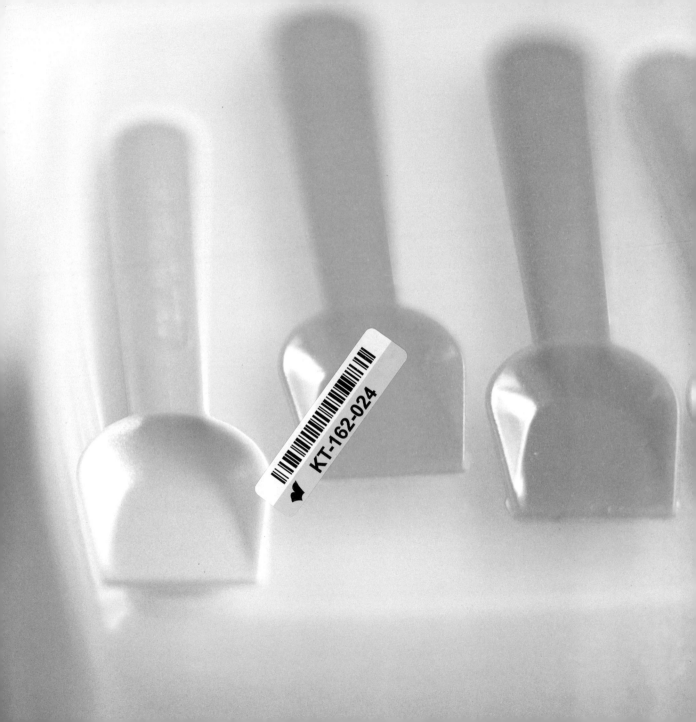

gelati
sorbets and
ice creams

gelati
sorbets and
ice creams

elsa petersen-schepelern

photography by

james merrell

RYLAND
PETERS
& SMALL

Art Director   **Jacqui Small**

Art Editor   **Penny Stock**

Editor   **Elsa Petersen-Schepelern**

Photography   **James Merrell**

Food Stylist   **Bridget Sargeson**

Stylist   **Ben Kendrick**

Production   **Kate Mackillop**

Note: Some of the sorbets and ice creams in this book contain raw egg whites, which have been added to lighten the mixture. If there is a problem with eggs in your area, omit them. In addition, uncooked eggs should not be served to the elderly, the very young, or to pregnant women. In all these recipes, the egg white may be omitted if preferred.

My thanks to Nowelle Valentina-Capezza, Sonia Stevenson, Clare Ferguson, Stella Shamwana, Norah Meany, and Tom and Jenny Merrell

First published in Great Britain in 1997
by Ryland Peters & Small
Kirkman House, 12-14 Whitfield Street, London W1T 2RP
www.rylandpeters.com
4 5 6 7 8 9 10

Text © Elsa Petersen-Schepelern 1997
Design and photographs © Ryland Peters & Small 1997

Printed and bound in China

ISBN 1 900518 19 8

A CIP record for this book is available from the British Library

gelati
sorbets and
ice creams

Gelati, sorbets and ice creams are now easily made at home, thanks to the wide range of ice cream making machines now available. But, even without a machine, you can still make these recipes. Just pour the mixture into flat freezer trays, allow it to part-freeze, then beat to break up the ice crystals and return to the freezer. Repeat several times – the more often you do it, the smoother the end result.

For gelati, it is safer to make the custard base in a double boiler, or in a bowl over simmering water, to ensure it doesn't boil or curdle. However, I always make it in a saucepan over a very low gas flame, and have never had a problem with curdling.

Shown right are the four main styles of ices in this book; Italian gelato, gelato flavoured with alcohol, sorbet and ice cream.

The recipes are inspired by flavours from around the world, including Italy, France, Scandinavia, India and South-east Asia.

6

gelato di crèma

A great basic Italian gelato recipe, made with cream rather than milk. It produces rather a large quantity, so divide the mixture into two or three parts, add a different flavouring to each, then churn each one separately.

1 litre whipping or single cream
5 egg yolks
250 g caster sugar

Pour the cream into a saucepan and heat gently. Beat the egg yolks and sugar together in a bowl until pale and creamy.

Beat 2 tablespoons of the hot cream into the egg mixture, then beat in the remaining cream, little by little.

Pour into a double boiler, or into a bowl set over a pan of simmering water, and cook over a gentle heat, stirring constantly, until the mixture coats the back of a spoon.

Cool, add your preferred flavourings, then churn, and serve or freeze.

Makes about 1.5 litres

italian gelati

traditional italian
gelato

Traditional Italian gelato is made with milk rather than cream, making it denser than French ice creams. However Italians, like all of us, love a good bout of self-indulgence, and make gelato with cream too, as you will see in the other two recipes in this chapter. Use any of the recipes in this chapter as a basis for the different and delicious flavours you will find in a Florentine *gelateria*. This one uses vanilla – and the minute black seeds in the vanilla pod give the best and most authentic taste and appearance. (Omit the vanilla if adding other flavours.)

2 vanilla pods

or ½ teaspoon

vanilla extract

500 ml full-cream milk

4 egg yolks

125 g caster sugar

If using vanilla pods, split in half lengthways. Place the pods or vanilla extract in a pan with the milk and heat to just below boiling point. Scrape the seeds into the milk and leave to infuse for at least 10 minutes. Stir well, then remove the pods. Reheat the cream to just below boiling point.

In a clean bowl, beat the egg yolks until creamy, then beat in 1–2 tablespoons of the hot milk. Beat in the remaining milk, then return the egg mixture to the saucepan, beating all the time. Stir in the sugar, then transfer to a double boiler or heatproof bowl set over a pan of simmering water. Cook over a gentle heat, stirring constantly, until the mixture coats the back of a wooden spoon. Do not allow the mixture to boil, or it will curdle. Be patient, and keep stirring.

Remove from the heat, cool, chill, then churn in an ice cream machine, or make by hand according to the method on page 6.

Makes about 750 ml

a **simple** gelato recipe – use it as a base for other flavours

500 ml milk

2 vanilla pods (see page 10), or

¼ teaspoon vanilla extract (optional)

3-4 egg yolks

125 g sugar

250 ml double or whipping cream

Italian gelato is usually made with milk, as on page 10, and so is denser than French ices. Made with cream only, as on page 8, or a mixture of cream and milk, as here, they are even more delicious.

Both nations produce great ice cream – though the Italians are generally thought to have the edge!

Omit the vanilla if using this recipe as a basis for other flavours.

Heat the milk with the vanilla, if using, until just below boiling point. Set aside to infuse for 15 minutes. Remove the pods. Beat the egg yolks until creamy. Whisk 2 tablespoons of the hot milk into the egg mixture, then beat in the remaining milk, a little at a time. Stir in the sugar, then transfer to a double boiler and cook over a gentle heat, stirring constantly, until the mixture coats the back of a wooden spoon. Do not allow the mixture to boil, or it will curdle.

Remove from the heat, dip the pan into cold water to stop the cooking process, then cool, stir in the cream, add any flavourings, churn, and freeze.

Makes about 1 litre

rich traditional gelato

gelato di strega

Strega is the Italian word for 'witch' – and for the flower-flavoured liqueur usually served after dinner. Always take care adding alcohol to ices – it lowers the freezing point and if you add too much to your mixture, it won't freeze properly. If you don't have any Strega available, you could substitute the orange-flavoured Grand Marnier. In Italy, they might also substitute liqueurs such as Amaretto or Crème di Cacao.

**500 ml *Gelato di crèma* (page 8)
or Rich traditional gelato (page 13)**
**4 tablespoons Strega or
Grand Marnier**

Make the gelato according to the chosen recipe. Add the Strega or Grand Marnier, then churn and freeze.
Makes about 500 ml

liqueur-

flavoured gelati

Tiramisu is probably Italy's most famous pudding, and beloved of those with a sweet tooth, wherever they live. It is the basis of this thoroughly wicked concoction. Sweet Marsala wine is the traditional flavouring, but rum could also be used.

Dip the sponge fingers in Marsala or rum, freeze, then dice.

Mix 3 tablespoons strong espresso coffee with the mascarpone, taste, then add more coffee if preferred.

Make the Zabaglione gelato on page 18, then churn. Remove from the ice cream machine and spread a layer of the mixture over the base of a plastic freezer box or loaf tin.

Dot with a layer of diced sponge fingers and a layer of espresso mascarpone. Cover with a second layer of Zabaglione gelato. Repeat as necessary, according to the size of your container, then place in the freezer.

Remove to the refrigerator for 20 minutes before serving, and decorate with whipped cream and shaved dark chocolate.

Serves 6-8

tiramisu
gelato

8 sponge fingers

sweet Marsala or rum (see method)

3-6 tablespoons strong espresso

coffee, chilled

250 ml mascarpone

1 quantity Zabaglione gelato (page 18)

to decorate

whipped cream

shaved dark chocolate

Variation:

Teetotal Tiramisu

Dip sponge fingers in espresso coffee, crumble, then add to 500 ml *Gelato di crèma* on page 8. Sprinkle with drinking chocolate, gently stir into whorls, then freeze. Serve in ice cream cones.

an amazin

zabaglione gelato

Zabaglione comes from the old Neapolitan dialect and means 'great foam'. It can also be made with other flavourings – in France it is made with white wine or champagne, and is known as *sabayon*, while in Spain, it is made with sweet sherry.

Alcohol inhibits freezing, so this gelato is quite soft, and may not need to be softened further in the refrigerator before serving.

To make the ice cream, place the sugar and water in a pan and boil until the sugar has completely dissolved. Remove from the heat. Beat the egg yolks until pale and creamy. Whisk 2 tablespoons of the hot syrup into the eggs, then gradually whisk the egg mixture back into the syrup – the mixture froths, like zabaglione. Fold in the whipped cream and Marsala, then churn and freeze.

Makes about 750 ml

150 g sugar

250 ml water

3 egg yolks

250 ml whipped cream

**6 tablespoons
sweet Marsala**

18

elato flavour, **wicked** with Marsala

flesh of ½ small, very ripe pineapple

3 tablespoons freshly grated

coconut, or coconut powder, plus

shaved fresh coconut, to serve

4-6 tablespoons caster sugar

6 tablespoons dark rum (see left)

2 drops vanilla extract (optional)

500 ml whipping cream or Traditional

Italian gelato (page 10)

The piña colada of gelati – pineapple, rum and coconut seem to be the very essence of the Caribbean. Make it as an ice cream, with cream, or as a gelato by mixing it with one of the basic gelato recipes. Serve at a sunny summer lunch in the garden.

Another wonderful flavouring idea is to place 2 vanilla pods in a small bottle of rum and set aside for 1–2 days before using. The taste is just like rum and raisin ice cream!

Purée the pineapple with the coconut and half the sugar. Stir in the rum and vanilla, if using. Taste, and add extra sugar if needed. Fold into the cream or Traditional Italian gelato, then churn and freeze.

Soften in the refrigerator for 20 minutes, then serve, topped with shaved coconut.

Makes about 1.25 litres

pineapple, rum and
coconut gelato

21

fruit and

Make these popsicles with any of the flavours in this book, or peach gelato, as below.

Place the peaches and sugar in a saucepan with water to cover. Bring to the boil, then simmer until the fruit is cooked but not too soft. Remove from the pan and slip off the skins. Cut in half and remove the stones. Boil the liquid until reduced to about 250 ml, then cool. Purée the fruit in a food processor, adding enough liquid to make 500 ml. Chill. Make the gelato according to the recipe on page 8, add the peach purée, then churn. Press the fruit gelato into plastic popsicle moulds, cover and store in the freezer. Unmould just before serving. If moulds are not available, use small plastic cups and wooden ice cream sticks.
Makes about 1 litre

500 g ripe peaches

125 g sugar

water, to cover

500 ml *Gelato di crèma*

(recipe page 8)

fruit popsicles

spice gelati

peaches in
sauternes
gelato

What do you drink with ices? Remembering that your tastebuds become rather frozen into inaction, it should be strongly flavoured and sweet, such as the sauternes used in this recipe, or perhaps a Bellini made with peach liqueur and champagne.

Make this recipe as a gelato or as an ice cream, according to taste.

1 half bottle sweet dessert wine, such as sauternes

200 g caster sugar, or to taste

6 yellow peaches

250 ml Rich traditional gelato (page 13), or 250 ml whipping cream to serve

sprigs of mint

1 ripe peach, sliced into wedges

Place the wine in saucepan, add the sugar, heat gently and stir until dissolved. Add the peaches in a single layer and poach them until cooked but not soft. (Turn them over when half cooked if the liquid does not cover them completely.)

Cool and chill, then slip off the skins, cut in half, and remove the pits. Place the flesh in a blender and purée with enough poaching liquid to make 750 ml. Add sugar to taste.

Mix the purée into either the gelato mixture, or the heavy cream, according to taste.

Churn and freeze. Serve, decorated with the sprigs of mint and peach slices, if using.

Makes about 1 litre

Variation:

Peach Gelato with Peach Eau de Vie

Poach the peaches as above, substituting water for the sweet wine, and adding an extra 2 tablespoons caster sugar. Add about 4 tablespoons peach liqueur while churning.

500 ml *Gelato di crèma* **(page 8) or**

Rich Italian gelato (page 13)

75 g passionfruit pulp, with seeds

4 tablespoons Galliano or Grand

Marnier, plus extra, to serve

4-6 ripe passionfruit, to serve

Make the chosen gelato and, just before churning, stir in the passionfruit pulp and Galliano. Freeze.

Soften in the refrigerator for 10–20 minutes before serving with fresh passionfruit, as described left.

Serves 4-6

Passionfruit and Galliano, the yellow Italian liqueur, is a marriage made in heaven. Don't buy a full-size bottle – just a miniature if you can find one, otherwise a half will last you through many summers. Use Grand Marnier instead if you can't easily find Galliano.

A simple, delicious summer dessert consists of a large bowl of chilled passionfruit in the middle of the table, a small plate for each person, with an egg cup and a teaspoon. Put a passionfruit in each egg cup, slice off the top, drip a few drops of Galliano into the fruit and eat like a soft-boiled egg. Bliss!

Serve with Galliano Kir – glasses of chilled champagne with a few drops of Galliano.

passionfruit
galliano
gelato

mascarpone is a wonderful
addition to any gelato recipe

mascarpone, cognac and
clove gelato

This recipe is just divine – so wonderful that I would recommend adding mascarpone to any of the *gelati* in this book! I have used rather a large quantity of cloves, because the flavour has to survive both removal of the cloves and freezing – and also because I love the taste of cloves. Use fewer if you wish.

Heat the cream with the cloves, set aside to infuse for 30 minutes, then strain.

Whisk the egg yolks and sugar together until pale and creamy. Beat in the cream, then cook over a gentle heat, or in a double boiler, stirring constantly, until the mixture coats the back of a wooden spoon. Do not boil or the mixture will curdle.

Cool, chill, mix with the mascarpone and cognac, if using, then churn.

Serve immediately or transfer to the freezer. If frozen, soften in the refrigerator for about 20 minutes before serving.

Makes about 1.2 litres

500 ml whipping cream

18 cloves

3 egg yolks

125 g caster sugar

400 ml mascarpone, beaten

1-2 tablespoons cognac (optional)

29

gingered poache

A variation on the traditional French recipe of pears poached in red wine. Serve the pears with either ginger gelato or the alternative ginger ice cream.

4-5 pieces stem ginger in syrup

2-3 tablespoons syrup, plus

4 teaspoons, to serve (optional)

500 ml Gelato di crèma (page 8)

or ice cream made from:

  2 egg whites (optional - see page 4)

  4 tablespoons sugar

  300 ml double cream

gingered poached pears

4 pears

300 ml Stones ginger wine

or 300 ml water plus 7 cm piece of

fresh ginger, sliced

6 tablespoons sugar

1 lemon, sliced

1 cinnamon stick

Purée the ginger and syrup in a blender or food processor. If using *Gelato di crèma*, mix the purée into the gelato, churn and freeze.

If making ice cream, whisk the egg whites until they form soft peaks, then whisk in the sugar. In another bowl, whisk the cream to a dropping consistency, then fold in the egg white mixture. Churn, then fold in the puréed ginger and the ginger syrup. Taste and add more syrup if preferred. Freeze.

Transfer to the refrigerator for 30 minutes before serving either ice.

To cook the pears, place the ginger wine (or water and fresh ginger) in a pan with the sugar, lemon and cinnamon stick. Bring to the boil, stirring, until the sugar dissolves. Peel, halve and core the pears, brushing with lemon juice to prevent browning.

Add the pears to the pan, cover and simmer for 5–10 minutes, or until the fruit is cooked but still firm. Remove with a slotted spoon, cool and chill.

Serve the pears with a scoop of ginger ice cream or gelato and drizzle with ginger syrup.

Serves 4

pears with ginger gelato

almond amaretto gelato

This is one of the most traditional of all Italian gelato flavours. You'll find it in *gelateria* shops across Italy – but this one comes courtesy of Nowelle Valentina-Capezza and her children, whose enthusiastic gelato road-tasting has been much appreciated.

chocolate

125 g crushed blanched almonds

1 tablespoon Amaretto liqueur

500 ml *Gelato di crèma* (page 8),

Traditional Italian gelato (page 10) or

Rich traditional gelato (page 13)

Make the chosen gelato and churn. While the paddles are turning, add the Amaretto and almonds. Continue churning, then freeze. Place in the refrigerator for about 20 minutes before serving.

Makes 750 ml–1 litre

coffee and nuts

white chocolate and nut gelato

The macadamia nut is native to tropical Australia, and is now grown commercially both there and in Hawaii. Use blanched almonds instead, if preferred. Make sure you use unsalted nuts for this recipe!

500 ml *Gelato di crèma* (page 8)

75 g shaved white chocolate, plus extra for serving (optional)

75 g sliced macadamia nuts, plus extra for serving (optional)

Make a gelato according to the recipe on page 8. Fold in the chocolate and nuts, then churn and freeze.

Place in the refrigerator for 20–30 minutes before serving, and decorate with extra chopped Macadamia nuts and a few shavings of white chocolate, if using.

Makes about 650 ml

chocolate, ginger and nougat make

great **gelato** textures

ginger chocolate gelato

Ginger and chocolate make one of the world's great food combinations–another of those marriages made in heaven. If you can't find good ginger chocolates, use stem ginger in syrup and add extra chocolate!

125 g ginger chocolates

125 g dark cooking chocolate, shaved

500 ml *Gelato di crèma* (page 8)

to decorate

chocolate curls

sliced stem ginger

Chop the ginger chocolates into generously sized pieces and fold them and the shaved chocolate through the gelato, then churn. Freeze until ready to serve. Soften in the refrigerator for 20 minutes before serving, decorated with chocolate curls and ginger.

Makes about 750 ml

gelato torrone

Torrone is the Italian version of nougat, used in this very traditional gelato recipe.

500 ml Rich traditional gelato (see page 13)

125 g torrone or nougat

crushed torrone, to serve

Place the torrone in a paper or plastic bag and crush with a rolling pin. Stir through the gelato while churning, then freeze. To serve, soften for about 20 minutes in the refrigerator, then serve in scoops, sprinkled with more crushed torrone.

Makes about 650 ml

A favourite recipe from Zambia in Central Africa, on loan from Stella Shamwana, a great ice cream creator.

4 egg yolks

4 tablespoons sugar

500 ml whipping cream

75 g dark cooking chocolate, chopped

nut brittle

groundnut oil, or corn oil

75 g sugar

6 tablespoons water

50 g pecan or macadamia nuts, roughly crushed

To make the brittle, place baking parchment on a baking sheet and brush with groundnut or corn oil. Place the sugar and water in a saucepan, stir well, and bring to the boil over a medium heat. Continue to boil until light brown, then add the crushed nuts. Pour on to the baking sheet, allow to cool and set. When set, crush the mixture and set aside.

Make the gelato mixture according to the method for *Gelato di crèma* on page 8.

Melt the chocolate in a heatproof bowl set over a saucepan of simmering water.

Cool, add to the gelato mixture, stir in the nut brittle, churn, and freeze.

Soften in the refrigerator for 15 minutes before serving.

Makes about 1 litre

chocolate pecan
or macadamia brittle ice

neapolitan espresso gelato

The Neapolitans make some of the world's greatest coffee – strong and black, a little like the inky coffees of Greece and Turkey. Any strong, good coffee suits this recipe.

250 ml whipping cream

3 egg yolks

250 g sugar, plus extra to taste

250 ml very strong, fresh,

espresso coffee, chilled

Heat the cream in a pan to just below boiling point. Beat the egg yolks until creamy, then beat in 1–2 tablespoons of the hot cream. Beat in half the remaining cream, then return the egg mixture to the saucepan, beating all the time. Stir in the sugar, then cook in a double boiler, stirring constantly, until the mixture coats the back of a spoon. Remove from the heat, cool, and chill.

Add the coffee, taste, and add extra sugar if required. Churn and freeze.

Makes about 1 litre

capuccino gelato

Capuccino is one of the world's favourite coffees. This ice cream version is a variation on its theme. Use *Gelato di crèma* or Rich traditional gelato (page 13), as preferred.

500 ml *Gelato di crèma* (page 8)

500 ml Espresso gelato (see left)

to decorate

6 tablespoons whipped cream

shaved chocolate

Serve in one of two ways. Either place scoops of *Gelato di crèma* and Neapolitan espresso gelato in glass coffee cups, then top with whipped cream and sprinkle with shaved chocolate.

Alternatively, work with the two gelati slightly softened. Place a layer of Espresso gelato in a *café-au-lait*-style coffee cup.

Top with a second layer of *Gelato di crèma*. Add a spoonful of softly whipped cream and sprinkle with the chocolate.

Makes 1 litre

sorbetto melone

Melons are tricky things to use in ice creams because their flavour can be very elusive. Choose one of the very highly flavoured varieties, such as orange-fleshed cantaloupe, the marvellously scented Charentais, the green-fleshed honeydew melon or the Galia, used here. Just make sure it is very, very ripe, highly scented and well chilled.

1 chilled, ripe, scented melon

juice of 1 lemon

4 tablespoons icing sugar

1 egg white (optional)

Cut the melon in half and scrape the seeds into a strainer set over a bowl. Pour any juice into the food processor, but discard the seeds. Scoop the melon flesh into the food processor with the icing sugar and the lemon juice. Purée, then chill until very cold. Beat the egg white, if using, until it forms soft peaks, then fold into the melon purée. Churn and freeze.

Makes about 1 litre

**sorbets
and sorbetti**

italian lemon sorbetto

125 ml water

250 g sugar, or to taste

grated zest of 2 lemons

500 ml freshly squeezed lemon juice

to serve

lemon shells (optional)

The world's most wonderful recipe for lemon sorbet – courtesy of my Neapolitan cousin! It is very sweet – so if your prefer yours with a tarter taste, reduce the quantity of sugar or add a beaten egg white. Filter the mixture before churning if you like, but many people like the extra zip of the lemon zest. When peeling the zest, for this or any other sorbet, make sure none of the white pith is included, or the sorbetto will be unpleasantly bitter.

A traditional way of serving this recipe is in lemon shells. These are made by slicing a 'lid' off the top of each lemon and removing the insides. Freeze the shells first, then pack them with the mixture and freeze. Serve folded in white napkins on small plates.

Boil the water, sugar and lemon zest in a pan, stirring until the sugar has dissolved. Cool, chill, then add the lemon juice. Strain if preferred, then churn and freeze. Soften in the refrigerator for 15 minutes before serving. **Makes about 900 ml**

Variation:

Lime Sorbetto

Substitute a similar quantity of lime juice and zest, and proceed as in the main recipe.

mandarin
sorbetto

Always taste the sorbet mixture before freezing, then add more sugar if necessary, remembering it should taste a little sweeter than you would like the end result to be. These three sorbets are my favourites – especially the one made with ruby grapefruit – slightly bitter, and gorgeous with Campari. Serve a selection of flavours for a sunny Italian-style lunch. Italians of course would eat this at any time of day, including during the *passeggiata*, when everyone takes an evening stroll through the town to show off their new clothes, new babies, new suitors – and to catch up on all the latest gossip.

500 ml freshly squeezed mandarin or tangerine juice plus 250 ml water, or 750 ml mandarin juice

grated zest of 2 mandarins

200 g sugar, or to taste

1-2 egg whites, beaten (optional)

Place the water, sugar and mandarin zest in a pan, bring to the boil and stir well until the sugar has dissolved. Cool, chill, then add the mandarin juice. Filter if liked, add the egg whites if using, then churn and freeze. Soften in the refrigerator for 15 minutes before serving either alone or with other sorbetti.
Makes about 1 litre

Variations:

Blood Orange Sorbetto

Substitute 500 ml of orange juice, preferably from red blood oranges, for the mandarin juice, and proceed as in the main recipe.

Ruby Grapefruit Campari Sorbetto

Substitute 750 ml ruby grapefruit juice for the mandarin juice and water, and add about 250 ml extra sugar. Add 4 tablespoons Campari (optional) after the egg whites, and proceed as in the main recipe.

45

serve a selection of citrus-flavoured
sorbetti for a **sunny**

italian-style lunch

Clockwise from left: Italian lemon
sorbetto (page 44), Mandarin sorbetto,
Orange sorbetto, and Ruby grapefruit
Campari sorbetto (all page 45)

blackberry
and raspberry sorbet

Scandinavia is 'berry heaven' – yellow cloudberries are used to make jam, and *jordbær* (strawberry) ice cream and sorbet is made from little, dark red local berries, dripping with ripeness. In Denmark, the sweetened purée from berry fruits is used as a sauce for puddings – I love it with Danish Christmas rice pudding and the sinful concoction of rum, almonds and cream called *rom fromage*.

In Italy, they make a similar sorbet from a purée of any juicy fruit – try other berries, such as mulberries, or a combination, such as the traditional summer pudding mixture of blackberries, black currants, red currants, strawberries and raspberries.

In Italy, typical choices would be nectarines (purée with the skin, which makes pretty flecks of red), white peaches or very ripe apricots. However, I find most apricots taste of cotton wool, and use dried soft apricots instead, soaked and poached in water with a little sugar until soft, then puréed.

500 g blackberries

250 g raspberries

grated zest and juice of 1 lemon

400 g sugar, or to taste

water (see method)

2 tablespoons Framboise (optional)

1-2 egg whites, beaten (optional)

Place the first 4 ingredients in a saucepan, bring slowly to the boil and simmer for about 2 minutes. Remove from the heat.

Strain into a measuring jug, pressing as much fruit as possible through the sieve. If necessary, add water to achieve 1 litre of pulp. Cool, and stir in the Framboise if using. Taste and add extra sugar if preferred, then chill. Fold the beaten egg whites, if using, into the berry mixture.

Churn and serve immediately, or freeze.

Makes about 1 litre

49

One of my favourite ices! This is really an English sorbet – made here from Coxes, the finest English apple. Use freshly extracted apple juice (any variety), or a good-quality, freshly squeezed, store-bought juice.

The quantity of sugar will vary, because the apples will vary in sweetness. Taste after 4 tablespoons, and add extra if you think it needs it (remembering that cold dulls the taste). Calvados is apple brandy – but you can use ordinary brandy instead.

1 litre fresh apple juice

4 tablespoons sugar, or to taste

grated zest and juice of 1 lemon

2 very red apples

3 tablespoons Calvados or brandy

Chill all the ingredients. Mix the apple juice with the sugar and brandy until the sugar dissolves. Core the apples but leave them unpeeled. Either grate them, or purée in the food processor. There should be little flecks of red peel in the purée. Quickly stir in the lemon juice and zest to prevent browning.

Add to the apple juice mixture. Churn and serve immediately, or freeze.

If frozen, soften for a few minutes in the refrigerator before serving.

Makes about 1.2 litres

apple **brandy** sorbet

Plain yoghurt gives one of the more health-conscious versions of ice cream, with a lovely lemony edge to the taste. If you're worried about eating raw egg whites, omit them in this recipe. Though the texture will be different, it will still taste heavenly.

yoghurt pineapple
ice with mint

1 small, very ripe pineapple

250 ml plain yoghurt

400–500 g caster sugar, or to taste

2 egg whites (optional)

2 tablespoons chopped

fresh mint leaves

Peel and core the pineapple and remove the prickly eyes. Whizz in a food processor with 400 g of the sugar until smooth and frothy. Remove to a bowl and stir in the yoghurt. Taste and add more sugar if necessary. Whisk the egg whites, if using, until frothy, then fold into the mixture, together with the chopped fresh mint. Churn and freeze.

Makes about 1.5–2 litres

asian flavours

orange and cardamom gelato

I'm afraid I've really gone over the top with the cardamom in this gelato – but don't worry, the final effect is fabulous. Cardamom helps enhance the orange flavour. Always use green cardamom pods. The larger black cardamom pods are also good, but they have a slightly coarser flavour.

Wash the oranges well in hot, soapy water to remove any waxy coating before proceeding with the recipe. Remove the zest lightly with a lemon zester, taking care not to include any of the bitter white pith.

To extract the maximum amount of flavour from the cardamom and orange zest, don't strain the mixture until just before churning.

**2-3 tablespoons
green cardamom pods
zest and juice of 3 oranges
250 ml milk
250 ml whipping cream
3-4 egg yolks
125 g caster sugar, or to taste**

Place the cardamom pods in a mortar and pestle, mash until all the pods have opened, then remove the green pods and mash the black seeds further.

Place the orange zest and juice in a small saucepan, and simmer gently until reduced by half. Cool, then chill.

Place the cardamom seeds, milk and cream in a pan, heat, then set aside to cool and infuse for at least 30 minutes.

Beat the egg yolks until creamy. Reheat the cream, whisk 2 tablespoons of cream into the egg mixture, then beat in the remaining cream, little by little.

Stir in the sugar, transfer to a double boiler, and cook, stirring, until the mixture coats the back of a spoon. Do not allow to boil, or the mixture will curdle.

Remove from the heat, dip the pan into cold water to stop the cooking process, then cool and chill. When all is well chilled, stir the orange mixture and the custard together, strain, then churn and freeze.

Makes about 1 litre

serve with other **exotic flavours** from South-east Asia

lemongrass
gelato

Lemongrass is one of the herbs typically used in Thai and Vietnamese cooking, and is sold in bigger supermarkets as well as Asian shops. Though it does taste of lemon, there is really no substitute for its elusive flavour.

6 stalks of lemongrass

500 ml milk

3-4 egg yolks

200 g sugar

250 ml whipping cream

Cut the lemongrass in half lengthways and bruise it with a rolling pin. Place in a pan with the milk and heat to just below boiling point. Set aside to infuse for 15 minutes. Reheat. Beat the egg yolks and sugar until creamy. Beat 2 tablespoons of the hot milk into the egg mixture, then gradually beat in the remaining milk. Transfer to a double boiler, and cook over a gentle heat, stirring, until the mixture coats the back of a spoon. Taste, adding extra sugar if preferred. Remove from the heat, dip the pan into cold water to stop the cooking process, then cool. Remove the lemongrass – by straining if necessary – then fold the cream into the mixture, churn, and freeze.

Makes about 1 litre

indian
mango ice

Indians are connoisseurs of mangoes and grow hundreds of different varieties. Some kinds are best used green, for cooking or making chutneys and pickles. Others, rather inelegantly known as 'sucking mangoes', are kneaded between the fingers, pierced at one end and the sweet juice sucked out.

The greatest mango of all, however, is the legendary Alphonso, which probably got his name in the former Portuguese colony of Goa, on the west coast of India. Alphonsos are sold in puréed, canned form in Asian supermarkets all over the world, and the flavour is so remarkable you simply can't improve on it.

If you can't find 'Senhor Alphonso', by all means try this recipe with a similar quantity of puréed fresh mango.

This recipe is delicious made with cream or yoghurt, and with papaya instead of mango.

4 egg whites (optional)
4 tablespoons caster sugar
250 ml canned Alphonso mango
purée, or fresh mango, puréed
250 ml whipping cream

Beat the egg whites, if using, until frothy. Gradually beat in the sugar. Mix the mango purée with the cream, then fold in the egg white, if using. Churn and freeze.
Makes about 750 ml

Variations:
Mango Yoghurt Ice
Use plain yoghurt instead of cream. Add extra sugar if necessary, then freeze.

Papaya Ice
Omit the egg whites and, instead of the mango, substitute about 500 g peeled and deseeded papaya. Purée the flesh with the juice of 1 lemon or lime and 200 g sugar. Mix with the cream, churn and freeze.

a simple fruit ice makes
a great **tropical** cooler

250 ml canned coconut milk

250 ml canned mango purée, or

mashed fresh ripe mango flesh

250 ml whipping cream

6 tablespoons desiccated coconut

(optional)

Chill all ingredients until very cold. Pour the coconut milk into a bowl and beat. Whip the cream to a dropping consistency. Stir the mango purée into the coconut milk, fold in the cream and the desiccated coconut, if using, then churn.

Makes about 1 litre

Variation:

Custard Apple Ice

Cut 1 large or 2 small custard apples in half, scoop the flesh into a food processor, but discard the skins and seeds. Whizz the flesh with coconut milk, churn and freeze.

Canned Alphonso mango purée from the recipe on page 58 can be decanted into a plastic container and frozen for future use, or used in this very quick and easy South-east Asian ice. If you'd prefer not to use coconut milk, use extra cream instead.

The flesh of the custard apple – also known as cherimoya – can be simply puréed with coconut milk and frozen into a spectacular tropical sorbet. Taste before freezing and add a little icing sugar if not sweet enough (probably unnecessary, because custard apple is very sweet).

thai coconut
and mango ice

almond and pistachio kulfi

India is one of the great ice cream nations of the world. Not surprising really, since the cow is a sacred animal there. Their other choice in the milk department is buffalo milk (just like in Italy), and buffalo milk is even richer and healthier than cow's milk.

Indian ice cream – kulfi – is made of reduced milk, which produces a distinctive cooked-milk flavour.

You can do this yourself (though it's very time-consuming), or use evaporated milk, available in canned or dried form. Or you can enrich ordinary milk with extra powdered milk. I give two methods here, including the traditional one, just in case you have a spare four hours! Use rosewater if you can find it – or vanilla. If you can find kulfi moulds, do use them – but any little cups will do instead.

To serve, roll the kulfi moulds between your palms, up-end on to small plates and serve immediately (they melt quickly).

250 ml mango purée or 1 tablespoon ground cardamom may be used instead of the other flavouring ingredients.

For the cooked milk:

(1) **4 litres full-cream milk, plus**

   1 tablespoon arrowroot, or

(2) **1 litre full-cream milk, plus**

   75 g powdered milk

400 g caster sugar

15 g shelled, unsalted pistachio nuts, blanched, skinned, and finely chopped

15 g blanched almonds, chopped

rosewater or vanilla extract, to taste

For the traditional method (1), pour the milk into a wide, shallow pan, heat to just below boiling point and simmer for 2–4 hours until reduced to 1 litre. Mix the arrowroot in a little cold water, then stir into the milk. Cook until the mixture thickens like custard.

For method (2), simmer the whole milk until reduced to 750 ml. Mix the powdered milk with 2 tablespoons hot water until smooth, then stir into the hot milk.

Stir in the sugar until dissolved, then cool and chill the mixture. Stir in the remaining ingredients, pour into moulds and freeze.

Serves 6–8

63

Index